# The Football Grounds of the Early 19
## Mike Floate

Published by Newlands Photographic, 71 Stones Cross Road, Crockenhill, Swanley, Kent BR8 8LT

Text and layout © Mike Floate 2014

All rights reserved. No part of this publication may be reproduced or copied in any manner without the permission of the publisher.

British Library Cataloguing in Publication Data.
A catalogue record for this volume is available from the British Library.

**Front cover**: A postcard of Goodison Park, Everton F. C.
**Back cover**: A postcard of Bramall Lane, Sheffield United F. C.

ISBN 978-1-900257-24-4

Printed and bound by Catford Print Centre

**Above**: Manchester City v Bolton Wanderers in the 1904 F. A. Cup Final with the old side stand seen behind.

**Above**: N. L. Jackson, author of *Association Football (1900)*

# The Football Grounds of the Early 1900s

The motivation for researching, editing and publishing this book was simple - I wanted to read it myself. I bought books from the early 1900s because they had great photos showing the grounds of the time. Fast approaching the age of 60 I have seen grounds change from the classic Leitch-designed Selhurst Park, where I saw my first game in 1964, with terracing giving way to mud banks at the top, to the current all-seater stadia.

Looking back sixty years before my birth takes us back to 1895, two years after the F.A. Cup Final was decided at the unsuitable venue of Fallowfield. The images of that game are among the first photos taken of a match or ground. Most of the grounds featured in this book were being developed or built in the 1890s to accommodate the increasingly large attendances at games.

### The Photographers

As a former Staff Photographer on the *Non-League Directory* I became increasingly aware of the names of the best photographers of the day. I especially noted two images taken at the Crystal Palace in 1905. The photos credited to Russell & Sons which I use on pages 22 and 23 show goalmouth action, the first with a younger photographer knelt down by the goal. This is clearly the son who then took the brilliant image of the Aston Villa goal on the opposite page. Searching online it would seem that the father was John Lemmon Russell, whose family were photographers in Sussex. Further research on the photographers will now be a follow-up task for me having completed this book.

Another name which crops up at games across a wide area is Howard Barrett of Southwell. His excellent action photos cover League grounds in Nottingham, Derby and Sheffield. He was an excellent sports photographer and the internet shows that he was a prolific photographer recording local scenes and people.

I found that he had been involved in The Great War. How sad it would have been for him to die in action but contact with a historian in Southwell gave a more interesting answer. He used his photography skills to good effect and along with his brother perfected a kite system which enabled them to fly their cameras over enemy lines and take aerial photos of the trenches and fortifications. He survived the war. I have been given the family historian's address to continue my research into his work.

### The Background

The development and organisation of the game of football is both well-known and well documented elsewhere, but the development of the grounds and stadia we see in this book is worth briefly revisiting. Football has been played informally for centuries with mob football continuing to be played to this day on Shrove Tuesday at places such as Ashbourne and Alnwick. Boys at public schools played their own versions of football, with Eton and Harrow schools still playing their own form of football.

Cricket had led the way in agreeing the laws of the game and establishing clubs. With the coming of the railways and the ability to play teams from elsewhere rules for playing football began to be formalised and agreed through the 1860s. When footballers returned home on leaving school or university the organised game is likely to have followed with clubs being formed. Friends from individual schools would also have continued to play together as Old Boys clubs. It was clubs like this that formed the F.A. in 1862.

All of this football was recreational but the desire to compete and win brought the F.A. Cup in 1872. Almost immediately the interest in watching as well as playing was established and the need to provide facilities for spectators began to shape the game as we know it.

The F.A. Cup was initially London-centred, with early rounds being played at the Oval cricket ground as well as the final tie, and was the almost exclusive preserve of the upper classes. Early entrants from elsewhere included Queens Park of Glasgow, and the cost of travel was at least in part borne by public subscription. The cost of running a club needed to be met and the best way of covering this was by charging for admission. Enclosed spaces were needed, entry to the fields was through the gate, hence gate money. Astute clubs then had money ready to spend.

League football was a logical step, with this development centred in northern manufacturing towns. The desire to beat local rivals meant that the best players were sought and the use of funds generated at the gate to pay these players brought about the professional game. Ensuring that those who paid were the only ones to see the game brought about the enclosure of grounds, and the need to allow all who paid to see led to banks and eventually terraces being built. Stands were provided for those richer people who preferred to watch in comfort and away from the more primitive facilities elsewhere in the grounds.

The South of the country was still coming to terms with Leagues and the professional game by the early 1900s. To understand how far behind the clubs in London were, compare Tottenham Hotspur's White Hart Lane ground with Aston Villa's Villa Park through the images in this book. The old-fashioned comparison of League football to non-League football was both correct at the time and can still be understood today.

By the early 1900s the majority of clubs in this book had established themselves at grounds which are in many cases still their home ground. A number have moved on to all-seated grounds but their old grounds are still well known. Birmingham City, Manchester United, QPR and Watford were still to make their permanent moves and QPR are the only club to have two grounds feature in this book.

Only Grimsby and Bristol Rovers are at present not in the Football League or Premier League, and only Gillingham and Leicester City had yet to adopt their current names.

In addition to the grounds developed by League clubs there were grounds and stadia built by amateur clubs and entrepreneurs who could see the possibility of making money from staging games. In this category we have Queen's Club, the Crystal Palace and even Stamford Bridge.

### The Books

The oldest book used as a source is *Association Football* by N. L. Jackson whose photo is on the title page. The author was well-known for being the founder of the Corinthian F.C. in 1883. He presents his book as a history of the game with a slant towards favouring the amateur game over the professional. He is astute enough not to ignore the Football League and its impact but even at this early stage in the game's history is looking back to a golden era already lost. The sixteen photos included in the four hundred plus pages are an indication of his view of the game with photos of the cloisters at various Public Schools as well as portraits of people heavily involved in the FA, including the author himself. The book contains excellent information but is not an easy read.

*The Book of Football* is well-known to those interested in the history of the game and especially those who bought *The Football Grounds of England and Wales* by Simon Inglis (1983). Inglis included a number of old images which I was amazed to see, and which were probably the inspiration for me to find out more about old grounds and to find further images, such as Birmingham City's Muntz Street.

*The Book of Football* was published in twelve monthly instalments, costing 6 shillings each, the price of admission for an adult to a League match at the time. A binding service was offered so anyone buying a copy of the book today will have a proper book, if well-thumbed through continued use and reference over the years. Mine is inscribed as it became a Christmas gift in 1923; a book already eighteen years old given as a gift! A mark of its importance all those years ago, and still of great interest (and value) today.

The photos are often printed within the body of the text and many action images are included. Around this time a number of weekly magazines and periodicals were publishing illustrated match reports and many of the photographs used are also found in this book. A number of the images also appeared in other publications at the time.

One such publication was *Association Football & The Men Who Made It* by Alfred Gibson and William Pickford, published in four volumes in 1905 or 1906; the actual date of publication is not noted in the books but it includes team photos which are noted as being from season 1905/6.

Writing in *The Independent* in 2008 Hunter Davies says "The four volumes of *Association Football & the Men Who Made It,* by Alfred Gibson and William Pickford (1905), are the best books on football ever written. They're the best produced, the best published, with the best photographs and best information". The combination of Gibson, a football journalist, and Pickford, an F.A. Council member makes the book both highly readable but at the same time authoritative. In addition there are a number of plate photographs printed to a high standard throughout the books and also smaller, but still well-reproduced, images within the text.

For the reader today these four volumes give the best idea of what football was like at the time: a mix of tradition, amateur and professional, League and Cup but without bias towards any aspect of the game.

### The Missing Link

The biggest surprise in researching this book was that nowhere in any article was the engineer Archibald Leitch mentioned. By 1906 Leitch had built stands for Sheffield United, Glasgow Rangers, Middlesbrough, Fulham and Chelsea. As *The Book of Football* was being published Leitch was working on developing Liverpool's Anfield ground.

Leitch went on to work on 27 League and Scottish League grounds, and his work is widely regarded as having provided clubs with facilities which were not only functional in providing good views of the games but also elegant and imposing to look at from elsewhere in the ground.

Simon Inglis celebrated his work in *Engineering Archie* (2005). Of the Leitch stands still in use the Stevenage Road stand at Craven Cottage is an excellent reminder of the timeless quality of his work, little changed since being featured in *The Book of Football* in 1906.

### Finally...

In the early 1900s the Football League had run for about as long as the Premier League has in 2014. The first chapter of Volume 2 of *Association Football & The Men Who Made It* is by William McGregor, who was a committee member at Aston VIlla and regarded as the person who brought about the formation of the Football League. He writes "People need not dislike the League system because the League, as we call it somewhat arbitrarily, has become an all-powerful combination of wealthy clubs to which the question of £ s. d. is admittedly the most vital consideration." Some would say this is still true today.

It is all too easy to look back on a golden age in football and be cynical about the money in both the Premier League and Football League. Working with the historic books in researching this volume I see that nothing is new and that even 110 years ago the differing views about the game didn't really matter. The game on the pitch, winning and losing and simply being in and appreciating the ground as a passionate fan is what the game is really about.

Mike Floate, Crockenhill, August 2014

# Public Schools, Representative & Cup Final venues

The importance of the Public Schools is often mentioned but rarely illustrated in books on football. Therefore the inclusion of photographs of four schools in *Association Football* by N. L. Jackson is significant.

*The Book of Football* also includes a chapter on Public School Football with photographs of both the Wall Game and the Field Game being played at Eton.

Remarkably all of the photos included of the Public Schools show views or buildings still recognisable today.

By the early 1900s the Oval as a football ground was a memory, mentioned but appearing only in drawings. The increasing crowds for the F.A. Cup Final, other Cup Finals and the International matches also being played caused the organisers to either find privately developed venues such as the Crystal Palace or Queen's Club, a club ground such as Hampden Park, or even use rugby grounds.

For me this section includes the most surprises and is hopefully of great interest to all.

**Above**: The Wall Game at Eton, with spectators taking a great interest in proceedings.
**Below**: The area by Forest School used for football. This is still open common land by the school in East London and the buildings in the photograph are largely unchanged.

# Westminster School
## The Pavilion, Vincent Square, London

**Below**: The pavilion at the Westminster School playing fields near to Victoria Station in London has hardly changed since this photo was taken for inclusion in *Association Football* by N. L. Jackson.

# Brighton College
## Eastern Road, Brighton

# Brighton College
## Eastern Road, Brighton

<u>Photo, left</u>:
The playing fields at Brighton College still look very much the same today as here, other than being surrounded by modern sports facilities, houses and mature trees.

The houses in the distance are on Freshfield Road. The stark chalkface was the cutting within which Kemp Town station had been built, the terminus of a short branch line which finally closed in 1971.

# Charterhouse School
## Godalming

<u>Photo, below</u>:
Charterhouse School can trace their records of football being played back to 1862, but forms of the game had been played for many years prior to this. The school attended the first meeting of the F.A. in 1863 and the Old Carthusians team won the F.A. Cup in 1881.

Football is still played in front of the school buildings as in the photo below taken circa 1905.

<u>Photo</u>: West

# Queen's Club
## Palliser Road, West Kensington

*Oxford University v Cambridge University*
*Photo: Hudson & Kearns Ltd*

# Queen's Club
## Palliser Road, West Kensington

The Queen's Club was established in 1886 with a large number of sports being catered for. The club still use the same site today but is now solely dedicated to tennis and other racquet sports.

The ground hosted a wide range of representative matches both in football and rugby, with crowds of up to 10,000 being drawn to the games. The Corinthian F.C. also played their matches here in their early years.

The photos on these pages show the ground at the west end. Both the pavilion and the building behind the end stand are still in use today. The British Pathe film archive includes clips showing a further large stand on the side from which these photos were taken.

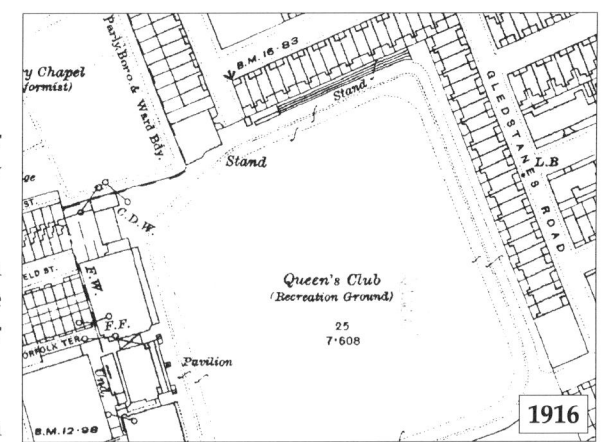

1916

**Right**: *The Book of Football* caption for this image reads 'Amateurs v Professionals at the Association game – The Corinthians v Southampton at Queen's Club.'

# Queen's Club
## Palliser Road, West Kensington

*Oxford University v Cambridge University*
*Photo: Bowden Brothers*

Already by 1905 when these images were taken, the main stand at Queen's Club looks dated. Built in two sections under twin canopies, with a small gap between, the south-facing elevation would have provided cover from rain but not the wind.

The whole ground, including this stand, can be seen on an image from 1928 on the excellent *Britain From Above* website.

*Oxford University v Cambridge University*
*Photo: Bowden Brothers*

# Queen's Club
## Palliser Road, West Kensington

The grand houses of Queen's Club Gardens were built in the 1890s to surround the playing area at Queen's Club. The small gardens between the buildings and the grounds gave a uniquely-enclosed venue for football. The residents must have been happier with the later use of the pitch area for athletics and eventually tennis than when football was played here.

The images show good crowds attending two of the representative matches staged at the Queen's Club. The Varsity match was staged here from from 1887 - 1921, after which the final was played at Stamford Bridge.

*Army v Navy*
Photo: Bowden Brothers

*Oxford University v Cambridge University*
Photo: Bowden Brothers

*Sheffield United v Derby County 1899*
*Photo: Cassell & Co., Lim.*

# The Crystal Palace
## Sydenham Hill

The history of the Crystal Palace ground is superbly documented in *To the Palace for the Cup* by Bevan, Hibberd and Gilbert (1999). They explain that the Crystal Palace Company developed an old fountain into a sports ground to enable the F.A. to be able to stage the Cup Final in London again having seen two finals played in Lancashire. A pavilion was flanked by two stands with cover for 3,000 spectators. The first final was watched by a crowd of 42,560.

The images here show the ground as originally developed, with the imposing Crystal Palace in the background. The ground was an inspiring, modern venue when first built, and a suitable home for the final tie to be played on.

Around the stands were the banks of the old fountain with flat standing for spectators at the side of the pitch and at the north end.

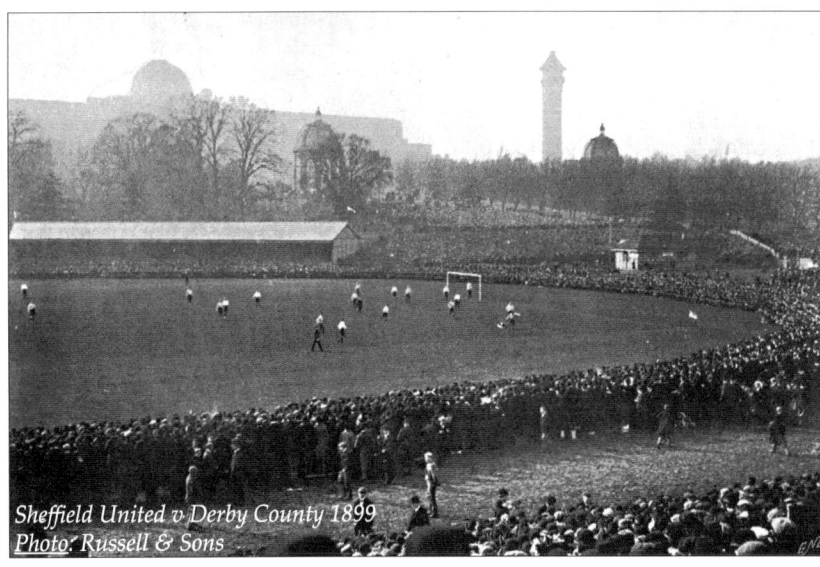

*Sheffield United v Derby County 1899*
*Photo: Russell & Sons*

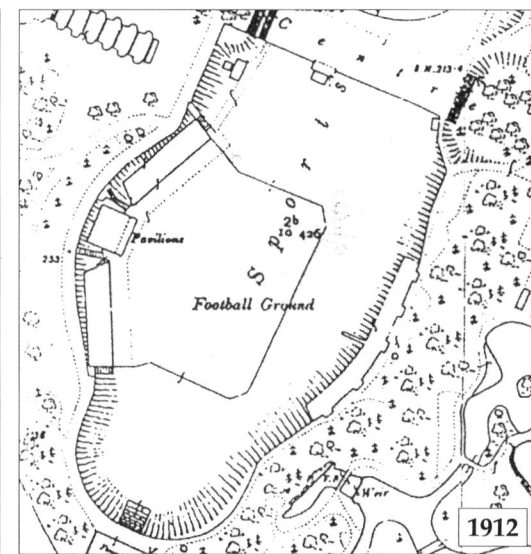

1912

**Below**: International matches were also staged at the ground. The stands flanking the pavilion were re-developed to seat an additonal 3,000 spectators, their gabled roofs enhancing the appearance of the ground.

*England v Scotland 1905*
*Photo: Russell & Sons*

# The Crystal Palace
## Sydenham Hill

**Below**: *The Book of Football* often used photos to illustrate articles. The caption to this photo suggests that using one's weight to charge an opponent off the ball is an effective way to tackle as part of a chapter entitled 'The Making of a Player, Half Back play'.

*England v Scotland 1905*
*Photo: Russell & Sons*

*England v Scotland 1905*
Photo: Russell & Sons

*Aston Villa v Newcastle United 1905*
Photo: Russell & Sons

*England v Scotland 1905*
Photo: Russell & Sons

# The Crystal Palace
## Sydenham Hill

Open seats were provided at the north end of the ground and can be seen in the images opposite.

Gravel terraces and open seats were built on the open bank opposite the stands and pavilion. These can be seen behind the action in William Foulke's goalmouth. Some spectators can be seen stood behind ropes approaching the pitch.

*Sheffield United v Tottenham Hotspur 1901*
*Photo: Russell, London*

*England v Scotland 1905*
*Photo: Russell, London*

Further photos show the ground opposite the stands and at the north end. Interestingly, it is often those taken at games with smaller attendances such as International matches which give us most information visually about the ground. The ground has received a bad press historically as a stadium for giving fans a poor view but clearly most spectators did have a good position for the game.

**Opposite**: The simple construction of the open seating area on the south side of the Crystal Palace ground.

**Lower, right**: *The Book of Football* caption reads 'Aston Villa v Newcastle 1905. Lawrence clears by a few yards a hot shot from Hall, but Hampton dashes up and scores the second goal for Villa.'

*Sheffield United v Tottenham Hotspur 1901*
Photo: Russell & Sons

*Manchester City v Bolton Wanderers 1904*
Photo: Russell & Sons

*Aston Villa v Newcastle 1905*
Photo: Russell, London

**Below & Opposite**: The father and son combination of Russell and Sons photographed a number of F.A. Cup Finals at the Crystal Palace. The image on this page would have been taken by John Lemmon Russell and includes his son, who took the image opposite. However, it is not known if the photographer by the goal is Arthur or Edward Russell.

*Aston Villa v Newcastle 1905*
*Photo: Russell & Sons, London*

*Aston Villa v Newcastle 1905*
*Photo: Russell, London*

Photo: Crawshaw, Sheffield

**Left**: The Newcastle United team before the Cup Final of 1904-5.

**Below**: *The Book of Football* declares the image to be of 'A famous Corinthian Eleven'. Of greater interest to us is the sight of the spectator accommodation with just a few spectators. The banks may well be packed earth but lines of barriers can be clearly seen.

Photo: Russell & Sons

**Right**: *The Book of Football* caption to the photo says 'The record crowd at the Crystal Palace in the Cup Final of 1900-1. This striking photograph can give but a faint idea of the actual appearance of the crowd of over 110,000 people which gathered at the famous Crystal Palace enclosure in April 1901.'

Not counted in the crowd were those viewing from outside - in trees and on rooftops, the houses of which are over the adjacent railway line, such was the interest.

Photo: Russell & Sons

**Below**: The images of the Wolverhampton Wanderers v Everton F.A. Cup Final of 1895 on this page and opposite are among the earliest surviving photographs taken of a ground or at a match. The official attendance was given as 45,000 but some reports suggest that up to 60,000 attempted to gain admission. It is clear from the photographs that the ground was too small for such a crowd.

# Fallowfield
## Manchester

*Wolverhampton Wanderers v Everton*
Photo: *R. Banks, Manchester*

# Fallowfield
## Manchester

Fallowfield as a ground is best-known for an F.A. Cup Final staged there in 1893. *The Book of Football* reports 'We were then at the beginning of the really big modern gates, and it is an admitted fact that the Association and officials who were in immediate charge of the game woefully underestimated the interest that the match was destined to arouse.

The Fallowfield Ground is an old one, and it did not possess the banking-up which modern grounds invariably have. There was, theoretically, space for a large number of people, but there was not room for more than 15,000 to watch the match in comfort. Fifteen thousand is quite an excessive number when they practically have to watch the match from the level.

The people were perfectly orderly for a time, but they could not see what was going on, and consequently those at the back grew restive. They saw a nice open space between the people close to the ropes and the players, and they naturally tried to get there. They pushed and fought, and then they threw clinkers and turf at the people in front. Finally the strain became too great for the barriers, which were frail, wooden palisading; they crashed in at many points, and soon there was wild confusion.'

1907

Wolverhampton Wanderers v Everton
Photo: R. Banks, Manchester

# Hampden Park
## Glasgow

**Below**: Opened in 1903, there is no better description than the ground's own website which says that when opened Hampden Park was 'the largest and most technically advanced stadium in the world'. Comparing the image below with the photos of other grounds in this book few are likely to disagree.

Photo: A. Porter & Co., Glasgow

# Hampden Park
## Glasgow

Hampden Park was built by the amateur Queen's Park club in 1903, the third ground the club had used with the same name. The importance of the club in the development of the game is indicated by the club website which reports that even before 1884 'the original Hampden... had turnstiles at entry gates already in place – the first of its kind at any sporting venue'. Today the club is a reminder of the past, in 1903 the ground was showing how a major ground should be built. No other British club has built a ground with a larger capacity since.

**Below, left:** A Scottish Cup Final at Hampden Park – Third Lanark v Rangers 1905. The match, which was won by Third Lanark by three goals to nil, was witnessed by 65,000 people.

**Below, right:** A Glasgow Cup Final – Celtic v Rangers.

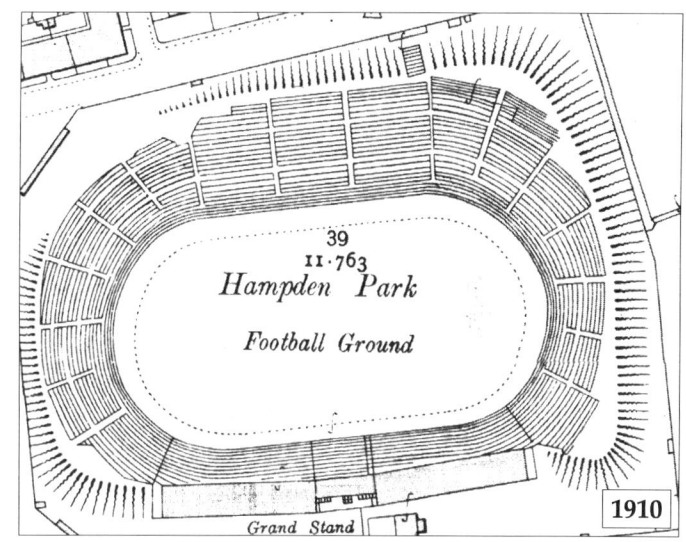

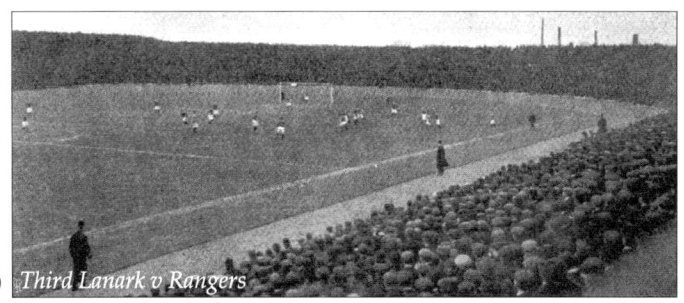

*Third Lanark v Rangers*

*Celtic v Rangers*

# St Helen's
## Swansea

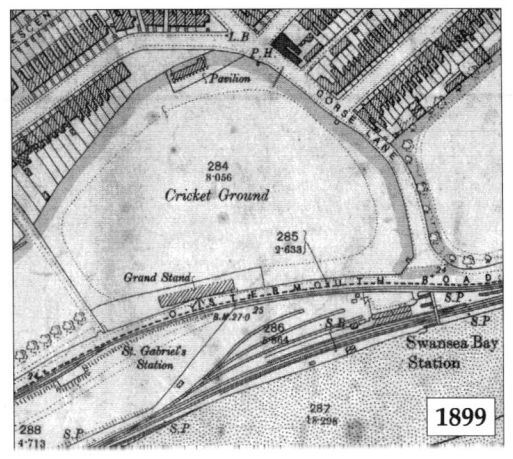
1899

The Football Association of Wales (FAW) was formed in Wrexham in 1876, and played their first International match against Scotland in Glasgow the same year. The first home fixture was in 1881. The FAW must have been looking to develop the game in South Wales when Wales played Ireland at the St Helen's rugby and cricket ground in Swansea on 24th February 1894. The attendance was 7,000, with Wales winning 4-1.

*The Book of Football* does not mention the game but includes this photo of the ground. No further football matches appear to have been played here until 1940 when Swansea Town, as they were then called, played here with the Vetch Field unavailable as it was being used by the military.

# Cardiff Arms Park
## Cardiff

The next International to be played in South Wales was on 16th March 1896 when Wales lost 1-9 to England at Cardiff Arms Park. The ground was used for five further International matches until the last was played in 1910, a 0-1 loss to England. Crowds for these matches are recorded as being between 10,000 and 20,000, impressive attendances for a sport not played at a high level in the area at that time. The superb stand in the photo below was a fine setting for these fixtures.

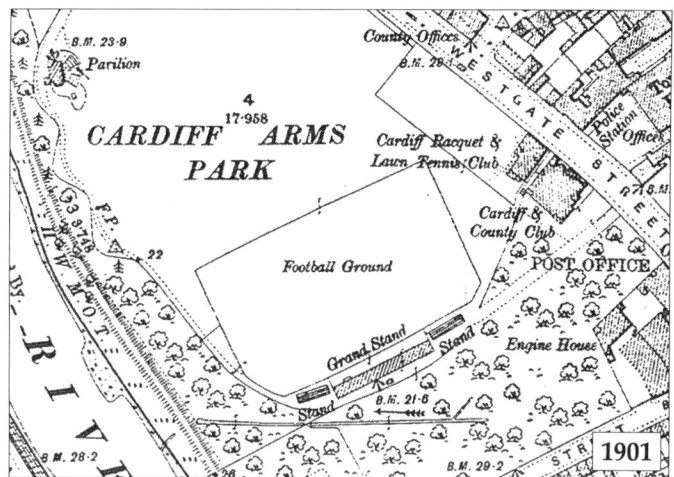

# Aldershot Military Stadium
## Aldershot

Photo: Gregory & Co.

# Aldershot Military Stadium
## Aldershot

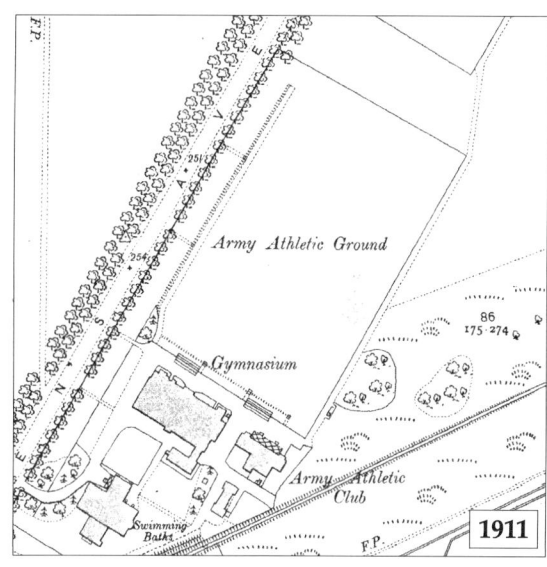

Football was also important within the military as noted already with images of the Army v Navy matches at the Queen's Club. For the Army the most important game in the calendar was the Army Cup Final. *The Book of Football* caption for the photo opposite reads: 'Easter Monday – a great football day at Aldershot. The Final for the Army Football Association Challenge Cup.

This annual contest is looked forward to with the greatest interest by the men who serve their King, and no more stirring sight can be seen than that presented at Aldershot on the occasion of the great Army Cup Final. The Challenge Cup is carried round the ground before the match so all may see it, and the twenty-two stalwarts are cheered on in the game by the rank and file who muster some 20,000 strong to do honour to the occasion. Last year victory rested with the 2nd Grenadier Guards, who defeated the Service Battalion Royal Engineers by 2 goals to 1.'

The Army Cup Final is still played at Aldershot Military Stadium and spectators see the match played out in front of an immaculately-mantained, classic pitch-length pitched-roof stand.

# The Football Grounds of the Professional Clubs

Reference is made in *Association Football And The Men Who Made It* to an early local Cup Final played in Birmingham which attracted a crowd of 5,000. The article goes on to say that at the end of the season the Birmingham F.A. had a balance of £100. Anyone who has been involved in running a club as I have will recall times when it seems that their local F.A. is more likely to be concerned with making money than helping the clubs in their area. I can well imagine the F.A. and local county associations, made up, as they were likely to be, of wealthy people not understanding the position of the professional clubs.

Each club needed to ensure that it had an enclosed area in order to charge for entry. As attendances increased the clubs would look to develop the ground, costing money. Cover for rainy days was also a consideration for clubs.

*The Book of Football* makes a number of references to clubs having problems securing grounds. The competition from builders for suitable locations as towns grew into suburbs caused a number of grounds to be lost to development.

In the early 1900s there were a number of grounds where the clubs had invested to provide excellent facilities. Of these Villa Park was the most impressive at the time, and along with Craven Cottage, Goodison Park, Stamford Bridge, Molineux, The City Ground, The Hawthorns and Hillsborough are at the time of writing still hosting football in the modern equivalent of what was then Football Leagues Division 1 and 2. Sheffield United fans would hope that Bramall Lane returns to this level soon.

White Hart Lane is probably the most changed of grounds, with further development planned. At the time of the publication of our source volumes the ground was a Southern League venue and the photos in this book show it to have been what we would call a non-League ground.

Of the other grounds eight are still used by the clubs featured with seventeen moving on (including the planned move of West Ham United). The images in this section are an amazing record of some great grounds. The photographers are deserving of our appreciation for their work.

# Aston Villa F.C.
## Villa Park

**Below:**
Aston Villa Football Grounds & Sports Enclosure, from a brochure produced to secure additional advertising at the Villa Park.

*Millwall Athletic v Derby County*
Photo: Bowden Bros.

# Aston Villa F.C.
## Villa Park

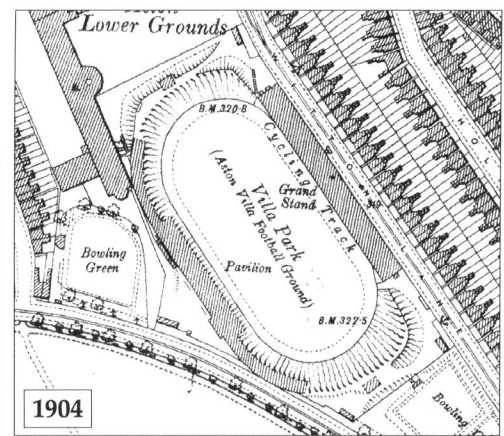

*England XI v Scotland 8th April 1899*
Photo: Gregson

**1904**

Photo: Howard Barrett

The map above shows how Villa Park in the early 1900s fitted well into the space available in the Aston Lower Grounds. The Witton Lane stand, with its barrel roofs, had been built in 1897. At the time architects had not settled on the most effective way to cover a grandstand, and even Archibald Leitch tried this form at Ayresome Park before settling on the pitched roof as being his roof of preference.

Villa Park was also used for athletics and cycling in the early 1900s, the cycle track lasting until 1913. With cover on both sides and good terraces this was a most impressive stadium for the time.

# Aston Villa F.C.
## Villa Park

**Below:** Villa Park was first used for an F.A. Cup semi-final tie in 1901. The image below shows a large crowd gathered for the second such game to be staged at the ground, in 1903. Villa Park was clearly a most suitable venue.

The photos show the slopes of the cycle track in use by football spectators, who appear to be seated. Trinity Road runs behind the stand and the Holte End follows the curve of the cycle track.

*Millwall Athletic v Derby County*
*Photo: Bowden Bros.*

38

# Birmingham City F.C.
## Muntz Street

Sadly *The Book of Football* article on Birmingham City makes no mention of the ground at Muntz Street other than naming it as the home ground, although there are some rather disparaging remarks about the former Coventry Road ground. This amazing end stand at Muntz Street was the image from *The Football Grounds of England and Wales* by Simon Inglis (1983) which made me stop in my tracks and resolve to find out more about old grounds.

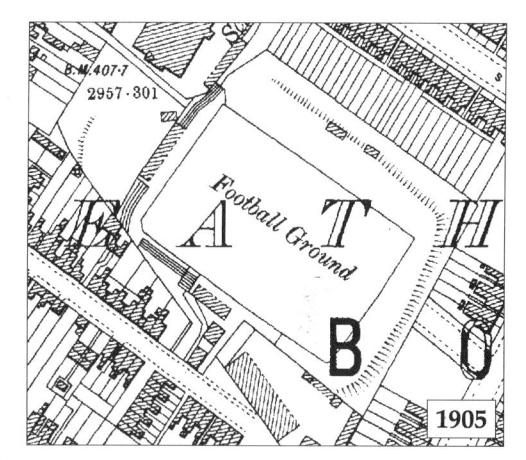

*Photo: Albert Wilkes, West Bromwich*

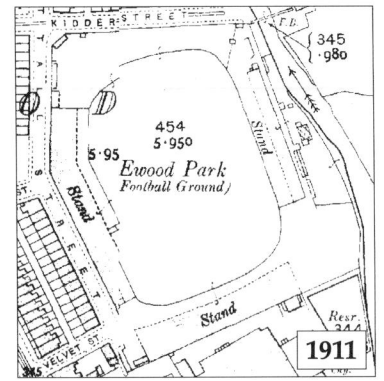

# Blackburn Rovers F.C.
## Ewood Park

**1911**

The *Book of Football* gives some background to this ground saying 'Ewood Park was taken over in 1890, and bought for £2,500 in 1893-4. The playing surface is one of the finest in the First Division. A fine covered stand was erected last season, and what is now needed is another with better-class seating accommodation.' It is interesting to compare the barriers on the bank with others at the grounds featured. The standard Leitch crush barrier had yet to be produced.

Photo: Hawthorn, Blackburn

# Blackpool F.C.
## Bloomfield Road

The caption in *The Book of Football* simply states 'The Blackpool Football Club enclosure at Bloomfield Road, South Shore, Blackpool.' The simple post and rail pitch-side barrier is the barrier of choice for many non-League clubs to the present day.

My memory of being given permission to take photos inside Bloomfield Road was that the touchline was higher than the field of play as well as having a sharp slope down to the cinder track. The groundsmen had apparently not begun the process when this photo was taken.

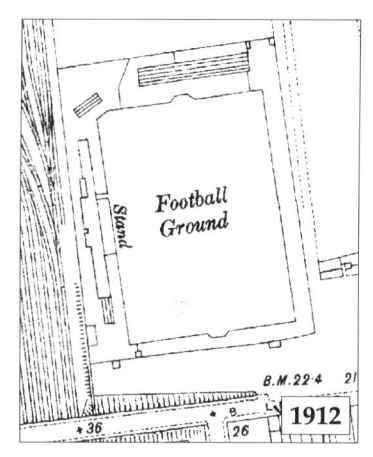

*Photo: J. P. Bamber, Blackpool*

# Bolton Wanderers F.C.
## Burnden Park

**Below:** *The Book of Football* caption reads 'The Last Cup Final played in Lancashire. Tottenham Hotspur 3 Sheffield United 1, F.A. Cup Final Tie 1901. T Morris, the right half, has just thrown the ball in from the touch line, and John Cameron and Erentz, the Tottenham right back, can be seen eagerly watching the flight of the ball'.

Tottenham Hotspur v Sheffield United
Photo: Bowden Bros.

# Bolton Wanderers F.C.
## Burnden Park

*Association Football And The Men Who Made It* describes Burnden Park as being 'a spacious and excellent enclosure five acres in extent, and capable of accommodating something like 35,000 people. The playing surface is dead level from end to end, but has a curious whale-back surface, so that those who are sitting at one side of the ground only have the upper half of players on the opposite wing in their vision. It is claimed that this formation is beneficial from a standpoint of drainage'.

The occasion caused bunting to be put out at the ground; note also the cycle track.

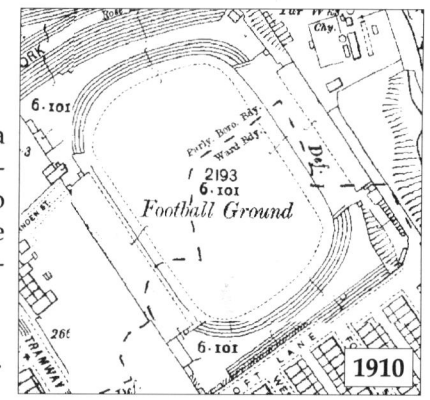

*Tottenham Hotspur v Sheffield United*
*Photo: Bowden Bros.*

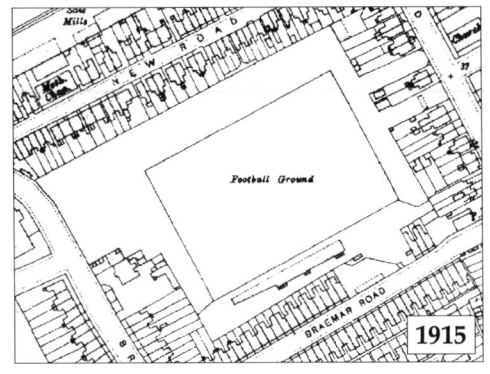

# Brentford F.C.
## Griffin Park

1915

Brentford appear in just one photo in *The Book of Football*. The caption to the photo is 'Brentford v Fulham, October 7th 1905. The Fulham attack, led by Wardrope and Fraser, is rudely repelled by Riley, Brentford's right full-back.'

The houses at the far end suggest that it is the Ealing Road end.

*Brentford v Fulham*
*Photo: Bowden Bros.*

44

# Bristol Rovers F.C.
## Stapleton Road

*The Book of Football* reports that the ground, later known as Eastville, 'was acquired by a syndicate. It was formerly used by the Harlequin Rugby team – that is when it was not flooded – and the Rovers laid it out to accomodate 20,000 people. The opening match was played there on April 3rd, 1897, when an Aston Villa team defeated the Rovers by 5-0. Last season a large portion of the banking was covered in on the popular side of the Rovers' ground, and a great deal more covered accommodation provided on the grandstand side. The Rovers now have accommodation for about 30,000, of whom a third can be placed under cover.'

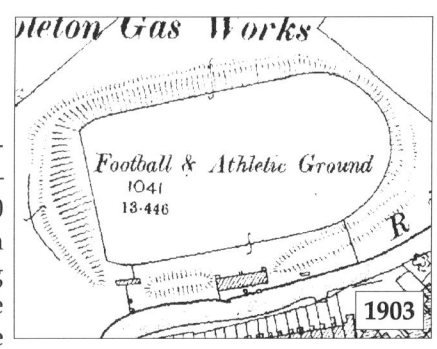

*Photo: Prothero, Bristol*

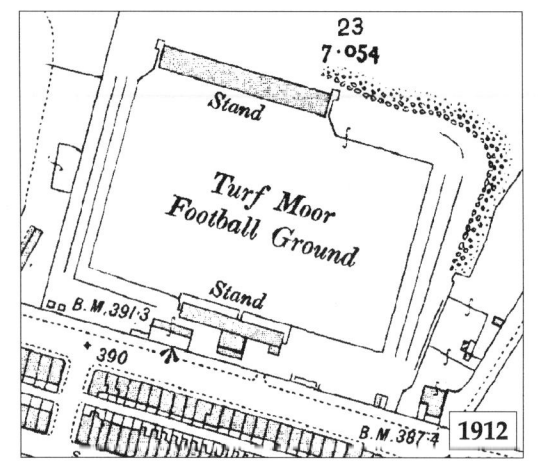

# Burnley F.C.
## Turf Moor

No mention of the ground at Turf Moor is included in the article on Burnley F.C. in *The Book of Football*. This is a great shame as the excellent photo below shows a good ground for the time, with stands on both sides and banks at both ends. The town centre location can be seen with both housing and industry seen behind the far end.

Photo: A. Greenwood, Burnley

# Chesterfield F.C.
## Recreation Ground, Saltergate

Sadly only the famous leaning spire remains from this photograph of The Recreation Ground, Saltergate, home of Chesterfield F.C. until 2010.

Photographers reading this book will be impressed with the wide angle lens which the cameras of the time had. One of the reasons I did not take photos at games back in the 1970s and 1980s was that the standard lens did not do justice to the grounds I was visiting.

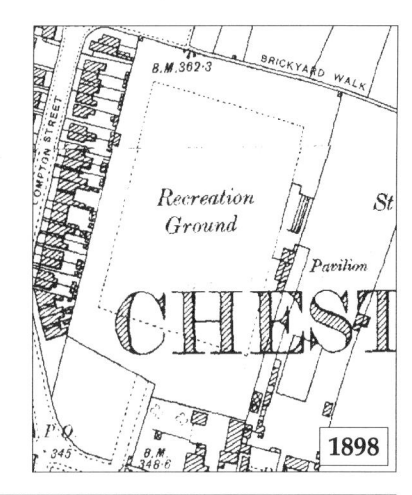

*Photo: Seaman & Sons, Chesterfield*

# Chelsea F.C.
## Stamford Bridge

*Photo: Baker & Dixon*

**Below**: The newly-established Chelsea team was built around their captain, William 'Fatty' Foulke, one of the first celebrity footballers. Foulke can be seen in this and other photos and is deserving of his place in the Index on p104. Reports from the time suggest that Chelsea employed small boys behind the goal to make Foulke look even larger than in real life as forwards bore down on goal. One such boy – the first ball boy – can be seen below.

*Photo: Bowden Bros.*

# Chelsea F.C.
## Stamford Bridge

Two years before the publication of *The Book of Football* the Stamford Bridge Athletic Ground was home to the London Athletic Club. The death of the freeholder of the land enabled Mr H. A. Mears to buy the ground, build the stadium and form Chelsea F.C. to play there. The writer reports that the grandstand was 120 yards long and held 5,000 supporters. The intention was to cover the far side in order to provide cover for 50,000. The club were especially proud to state that every spectator would enjoy an uninterrupted view of the game. The cinder track which was a distinctive feature of the ground until recent years enabled the London Athletic Club to continue to use the ground.

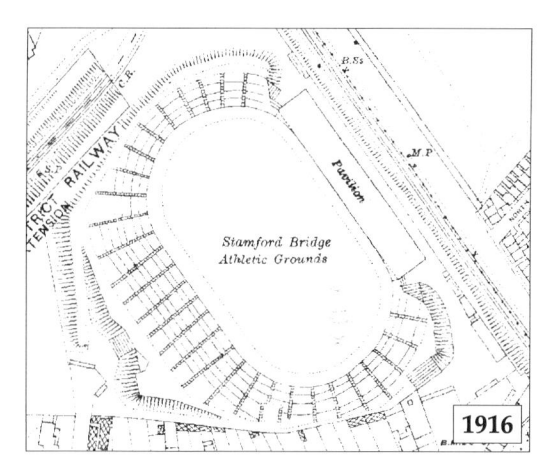

1916

*Photo: Bowden Bros.*

# Derby County F.C.
## The Baseball Ground

**Left**: The caption with this image in *Association Football & The Men Who Made It* by Gibson and Pickford is 'Cup tie crowd at Derby'. The ground is not identified but the factory behind the fans confirms it to be the Baseball Ground.

**Below, Left**: *Association Football & The Men Who Made It* by Alfred Gibson and William Pickford again has a limited caption 'An Attack on Goal'. This is likely to be Sheffield Utd v Aston Villa, F.A. Cup Semi Final replay 11/4/01.

*Derby v Bury*
Photo: Bloomer

50

# Derby County F.C.
## The Baseball Ground

Another caption without the writer formally identifying the ground appears in *Association Football & The Men Who Made It*. The caption to the photo below is 'A Sixpenny Bank' and was included as a stock photo within a chapter on *The Enthusiast in Football*.

With little to go on from the photo it was only when seeing the map, right, that I could be sure that the curved building behind the terrace was the Baseball Hotel and therefore the ground the Baseball Ground. With the images opposite also identified my source books give a better illustration of the ground at the time than they seemed to on first reading.

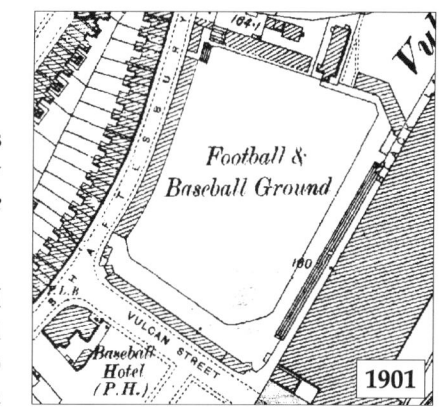

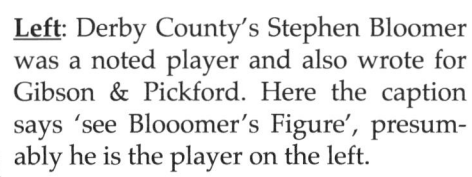

**Left**: Derby County's Stephen Bloomer was a noted player and also wrote for Gibson & Pickford. Here the caption says 'see Blooomer's Figure', presumably he is the player on the left.

# Everton F.C.
## Goodison Park

*Photo: Starfield & Co.*

**Below**: *The Book of Football* estimates the capacity as 55,000, and the uninterrupted view for spectators is highlighted. Among many figures included for various items of expenditure the total cost of £27,000 is sufficient to quote here. St. Luke's church can be seen in the corner of the ground.

The two photos show that in 1905 Goodison Park, along with Villa Park, was one of the most impressive of the Football League club grounds then in use.

*Photo: Starfield & Co.*

# Everton F.C.
## Goodison Park

Everton F.C. proudly claim that Goodison Park was the first major football stadium to be built in England. *The Book of Football* however makes no such claim but does detail the club's use of Stanley Park, a field at Priory Road and then Anfield, which it describes as being 'fully equipped for football'.

Goodison Park was first used by Everton in 1892 and by the following season the club had developed an excellent facility. In noting the spending of £3,000 on erecting a magnificent boardroom and suite of offices the priorities of *The Book of Football*'s writer are made clear.

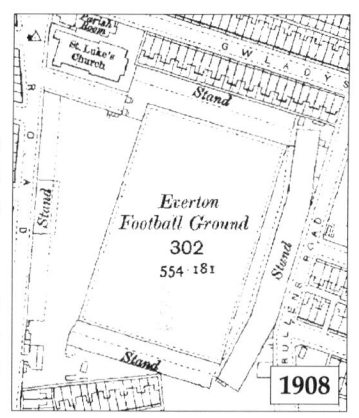

*Photo: Starfield & Co.*

# Fulham F.C.
## Craven Cottage

**Left**: The teams in the International Trial Match, Amateurs v Professionals of the South, played at Craven Cottage on January 8th 1906.

*Photo: Moyse, Putney*

*Photo: Moyse, Putney*

# Fulham F.C.
## Craven Cottage

Fulham F.C. had a number of grounds, detailed in *The Book of Football*, before settling at Craven Cottage. The article says 'the grandstand is 120 yards in length, the terracing quite perfect, and that the eastern end, not fully shown in the photograph, rises over eighty tiers in height, and when packed with spectators presents a spectacle imposing to a degree. The ground has the additional advantage of placing the spectators close to the field of play.' No mention is made of the short-lived wooden stand condemned as dangerous even in the early 1900s.

Photo: Moyse, Putney

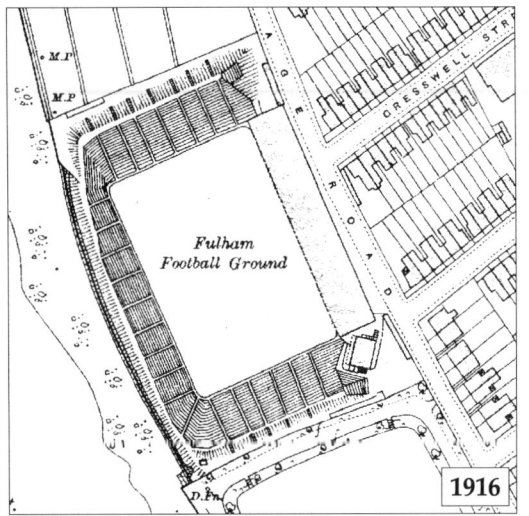

# Fulham F.C.
## Craven Cottage

**Below**: Fulham F.C. 1905-6, with the classic Leitch grandstand in the background.

**Below, left**: *Association Football & The Men Who Made It* include this portrait of J. S. Fryer, the Captain of Fulham F.C.. It is not clear exactly where the photo was taken but the far end does appear to be a bank or terrace. The stand-end seen behind the player is not Fulham's stand but he could be stood in front of an early dugout.

*Photo: Moyse, Putney*

56

# Grimsby Town F.C.
## Blundell Park

The image below is not captioned in *Association Football & The Men Who Made It* other than mentioning that Stoke are defending their goal. Fortunately I have another publication from the time which has the same image in a report on Grimsby v Stoke from October 1902, and so the ground can be identified as Blundell Park.

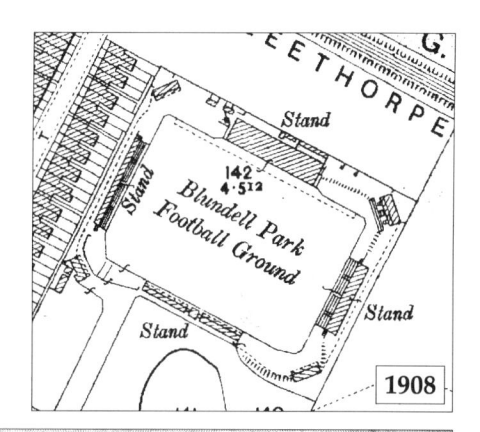

*Grimsby Town v Stoke City*
Photo: Howard Barrett, Southwell

**Below**: Leicester Fosse F.C. 1905-6, the photo being taken at the Filbert Street end of the ground. The terrace behind appears to be a simple structure made from wood.

# Leicester Fosse F.C.
## Filbert Street

*Photo: J. Herbert Wilson, Leicester*

# Leicester Fosse F.C.
## Filbert Street

The article on Leicester Fosse in *The Book of Football* includes the excellent groundview below. The image left is an unidentified stock image from *Association Football & The Men Who Made It*. Luckily the unique club name board on the stand identifies the ground for us.

At the time the club were still playing in the Second Division and the ground had yet to be fully developed.

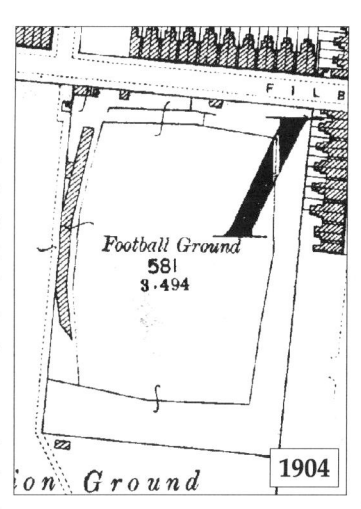

*Photo: J. Herbert Wilson, Leicester*

# Luton Town F.C.
## Ivy Road

*Luton Town F.C. 1905-6*
*Photo: W. H. Cox, Luton*

**Below**: The stand seen in the photo is likely to be the one brought from their previous Dunstable Road ground, just a few hundred yards to the south. The tall advertsiements at the ends enabled the ground to fit into the small space available between the existing houses.

Ivy Road, the original name, is behind the stand opposite. The newly-built stand with the gabled press box would appear to be on this side.

*Luton v Portsmouth*
*Photo: W. H. Cox, Luton*

60

# Luton Town F.C.
## Ivy Road

Writing in *The Book of Football* Charles Green discusses the advent of professionalism, and whether Luton were rightly to be considered the first in the South to pay players. Little is said about their grounds and just a brief statement that the club had recently moved ground. Green does say 'a thoroughly up-to-date ground has been fitted up' and that 'on both Christmas Day and Boxing Day a crowd of 10,000 gladdened the hearts of the officials'.

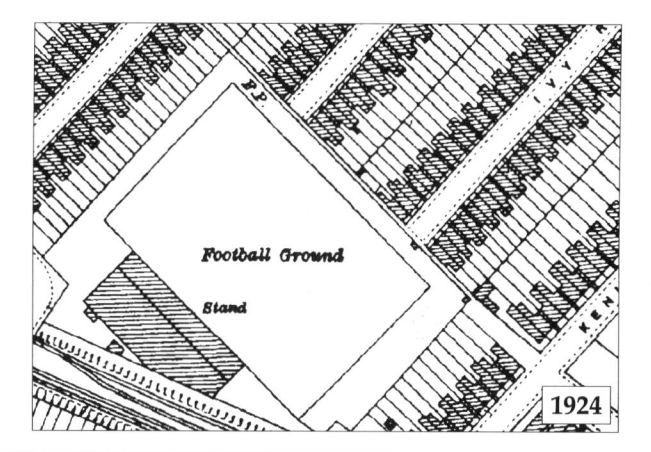

*Luton v Millwall*
Photo: W. H. Cox, Luton

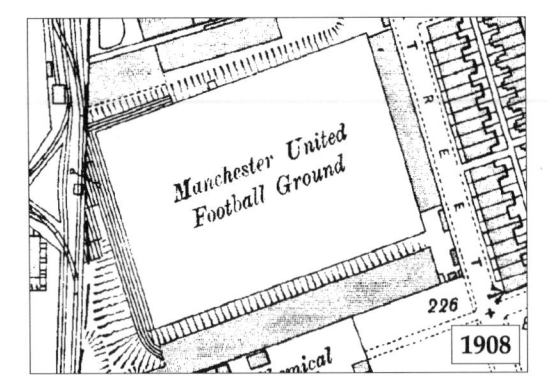

# Manchester United F.C.
## Bank Street

In an uncredited article on Football in Manchester the *Association Football & The Men Who Made It* author says 'It is not easy to picture the genesis of what is now the Manchester United Club. To-day at Clayton one sees palatial stands, twentieth century appointments everywhere, a highly paid team, tremendous throngs of enthusiasts, and an almost lavishly framed whole. It is necessary to go back to far-off days for the contrasting scene, and to imagine a little roped enclosure in which a thin ring of spectators stood watching a troupe of players in nondescript jerseys. Both players and watchers were humble railway workers, whose hearts were in the game, and whose only thought was of victory.'

He goes on to write 'The North Road enclosure… was the property of the Dean and Canons of Manchester, and one day these well meaning people came along with the impossible demand that no charge should be made for admission to matches. The club could not agree to this, the Dean and Canons were adamant, and notice to quit was issued. Bank Lane, Clayton, the present home of Manchester United, was secured, and from a muddy waste it has now become an enclosure of top class.'

# Middlesbrough F.C.
## Ayresome Park

The article on Middlesbrough in *The Book of Football* again omits to mention the engineer Archibald Leitch's work here but does say 'a capital site was selected in a residential part of town on the Ayresome estate, and to which an excellent service of tramcars run incessantly throughout the day. This ground… is a splendid enclosure, judiciously apportioned, and contains all the adjuncts to an up-to-date club and ground. It is capable of accommodating between 35,000 and 45,000 people, and cost between £10,000 and £11,000.'

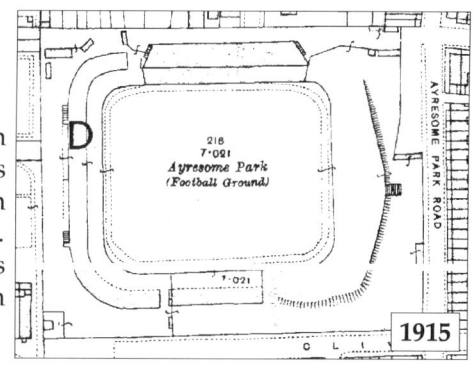

*Photo*: R. E. Fairclough

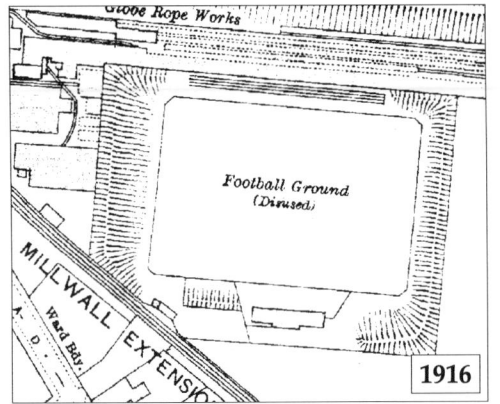

# Millwall F.C.
## North Greenwich Ground

1916

Prior to their move across the Thames to the Den in Bermondsey in 1910 Millwall played at four grounds on the Isle of Dogs. The team photo, left, was taken at the Athletic Ground, East Ferry Road, when the club were named Millwall Athletic. The club moved to the North Greenwich ground in 1901 and the action photo below was taken on March 7th 1903 during the club's 1-0 defeat of Everton in the F.A. Cup Quarter Final. The open seated area in the photo is on the north side of the ground. The club dropped the Athletic from their name at the end of the 1902/3 season.

*Photo: R. W. Thomas, Cheapside*

*Millwall v Everton*
*Photo: Bowden Bros.*

# New Brompton F.C.
## Priestfield Road

There was an historic interest in football in the Medway towns with the Royal Engineers club being based locally. *The Book of Football* notes that they played on open ground at the Great Lines. New Brompton Excelsiors, the club from which New Brompton F.C. was formed as a limited company in 1893, also played there. An enclosed ground was needed so as to be able to take money at the gate.

The photo below shows the Gordon Road stand, built in 1899, to the right, still in use in 1985 when the fire at Bradford City caused it to be closed. The club is the only one in this book to adopt a different name after the publication of the books used as reference for this volume.

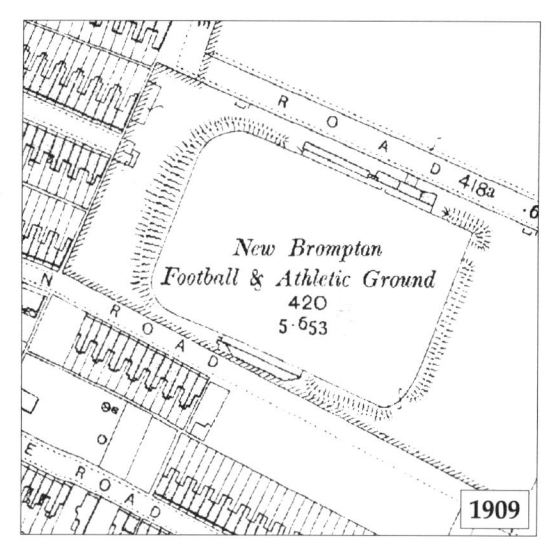

# Notts County F.C.
## Trent Bridge

**Left**: The prolific Southwell-based photographer Howard Barrett has two team photos included in *Association Football & The Men Who Made It* with the same stand behind the players. Here we have the Blackburn Rovers team but the caption does not record the ground at which the photo was taken. Research would suggest that the image was taken at the southern end of Trent Bridge.

*Photo: Howard Barrett, Southwell*

**Left**: Howard Barrett did not neglect the home team and took this excellent team group. Interesting for us is the background with the terrace at the northern end of the ground visible. The mature trees and the large Victorian villas on the Radcliffe Road make for a mix of old and new.

*Photo: Howard Barrett, Southwell*

# Notts County F.C.
## Trent Bridge

Even in 1905 the shared use of cricket grounds by football clubs was rare in the Football League, with just Notts County and Sheffield United being featured in this book and playing at such grounds.

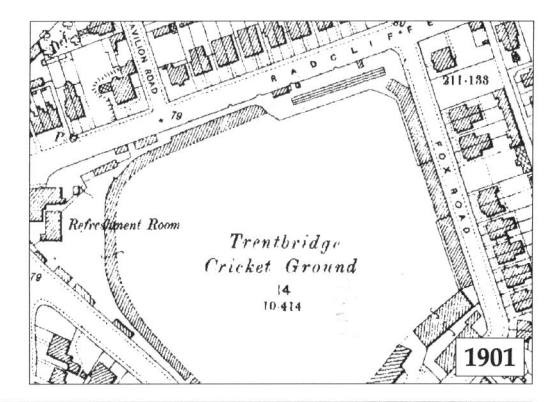

County were fortunate that Trent Bridge had a side away from the cricket square which was square at one end and offset at an angle at the other giving a good view. BFI archve film shows crowds along the fourth side with stepped accommodation for the spectators close to the touchline.

1901

*Notts County v Middlesbrough*
Photo: Howard Barrett, Southwell

*Nottingham Forest v Derby County*
<u>Photo</u>: *Howard Barrett, Southwell*

*Aston Villa v Everton*
<u>Photo</u>: *Bowden Bros.*

# Notts County F.C.
## Trent Bridge

Even in 1905 the shared use of cricket grounds by football clubs was rare in the Football League, with just Notts County and Sheffield United being featured in this book and playing at such grounds.

County were fortunate that Trent Bridge had a side away from the cricket square which was square at one end and offset at an angle at the other giving a good view. BFI archve film shows crowds along the fourth side with stepped accommodation for the spectators close to the touchline.

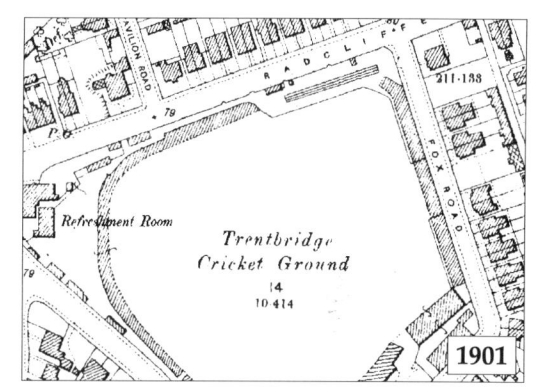

Notts County v Middlesbrough
Photo: Howard Barrett, Southwell

*Nottingham Forest v Derby County*
*Photo: Howard Barrett, Southwell*

*Aston Villa v Everton*
*Photo: Bowden Bros.*

# Nottingham Forest F.C.
## The City Ground

As is often the case in *The Book of Football* there is little or no mention of the ground in the Nottingham Forest article. Interestingly the club is referred to both as Notts Forest and the correct club name.

The City Ground can be seen to have been one of the better grounds at the time with good accommodation for spectators both in grandstands and on the terraces.

The ground had stands with paddocks on both sides with a small stand behind the goal at the Trent End. The other end was banked for standing spectators.

**Top, left**: *The Book of Football* notes that this Howard Barrett photo was of a local derby between Nottingham Forest and Derby County in a League match.

**Bottom, left**: The City Ground first hosted an F.A. Cup semi final in 1901. The third such game was between Aston Villa and Everton in 1905.

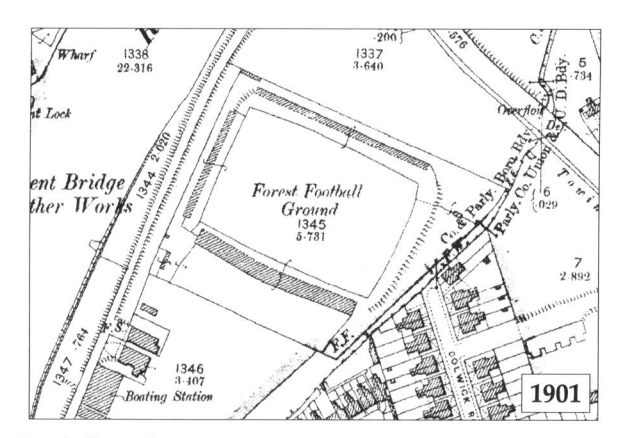

**Below**: The *Association Football & The Men Who Made It* simply notes 'A throw in'. The game is Nottingham Forest v Preston North End.

# Nottingham Forest F.C.
## The City Ground

**Left**: Local photographer Howard Barrett was out early to take this photograph of the crowds crossing the River Trent on their way to the replayed F.A. Cup semi-final between Aston Villa and Everton at the City Ground on 29th March 1905.

**Below**: Howard Barrett later took this excellent action photo of Aston Villa forward Joe Bache on the attack. The stand behind the goal is at the Trent End of the ground.

*Photo: Howard Barrett, Southwell*

*Aston Villa v Everton*
*Photo: Howard Barrett, Southwell*

70

# Portsmouth F.C.
## Fratton Park

**Below**: *The Book of Football* includes a team photo of Portsmouth F.C. in season 1905-6. Of interest today is the glimpse of the stand behind the team which would appear to be on north side of the ground.

*Photo: Stephen Cribb, Southsea*

# Portsmouth F.C.
## Fratton Park

**Left**: An informative article in *The Book of Football* includes interesting information on a key part of Fratton Park saying 'last summer a very fine clubhouse was erected over the main entrance in Frogmore Road, with board-room, manager's office, reading and card room, and billiard - room for the players with spacious lavatories and bar.' Note that the end of the main stand can be seen. The later Leitch grandstand was built over part of this pavilion, the rest can still be seen approaching the ground along Frogmore Road.

*Photo: Stephen Cribb, Southsea*

*Photo: Stephen Cribb, Southsea*

# Portsmouth F.C.
## Fratton Park

*The Book of Football* says of Fratton Park 'The embankments round the playing pitch have year by year been built up, and now provide accommodation for a big crowd, and during this summer have been terraced, thereby enabling everyone of the 30,000 which the ground is capable of holding to have a good view.' The accompanying photos show the ground to be on the rural edge of Portsmouth, with a good crowd making use of the new terraces.

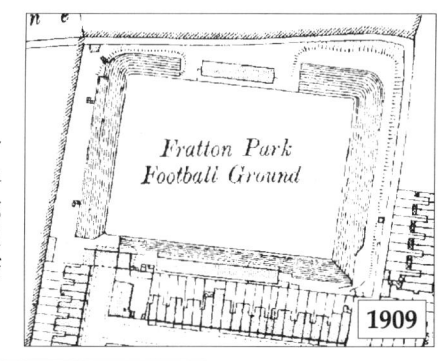

*Photo: Stephen Cribb, Southsea*

# Plymouth Argyle F.C.
## Home Park

**Below**: In a caption to this photo *The Book of Football* says 'The ground at Home Park, situated about a mile and a half from Plymouth, is recognised as one of the best and prettiest in the South. It will accommodate 25,000 people, and is capable of unlimited extension.'

# Plymouth Argyle F.C.
## Home Park

The *Book of Football* is an excellent historical document but is not great at recording history. In the article on Plymouth Argyle brief mention is made of rugby having been the dominant sport in the area but not that Home Park was owned by the Argyle Athletic Club or had previously hosted a rugby club. The rich history of the club, even at this early stage, is left for us to read elsewhere, with space given to details of the manager appointed on the club turning professional, and the players signed for the coming season.

The ground is seen in the photos to be open, with shallow enclosing slopes with a bank at one end providing spectators with a raised position from which to watch.

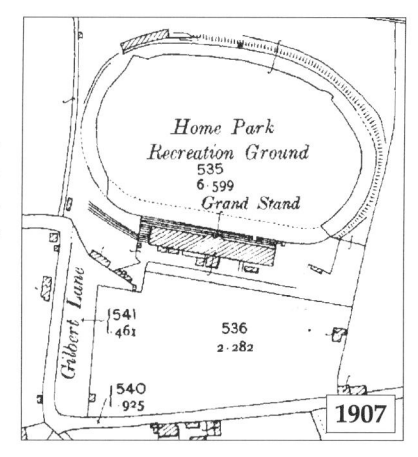

*Plymouth Argyle v Southampton*

*QPR v Southampton*
*Photo: Bowden Bros.*

# Queens Park Rangers F.C.
## Kensal Rise Athletic Stadium

The only club to have two grounds feature in this book, QPR are seen playing at the Kensal Rise Athletic Stadium, originally known as the National Athletic Ground. By 1908 the ground was home to Hendon F.C. and appears to have survived until cleared for the houses of Liddell Gardens & Whitmore Gardens to be built in 1921.

Tim Grose's website *UK Running Track Directory* reports that the ground opened on 26th May 1890 and had a grandstand with a capacity of 1000. These images are very rare examples of photos taken at the ground.

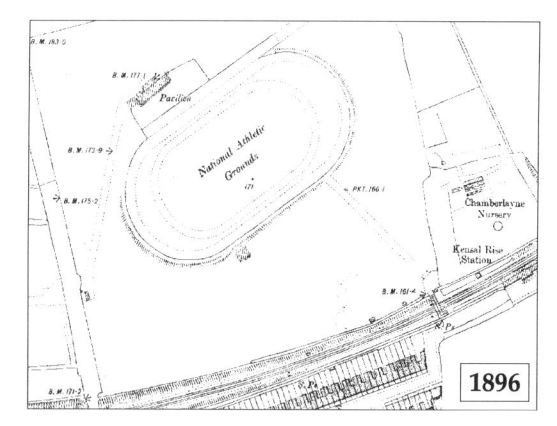

1896

*QPR v Southampton*
*Photo: Bowden Bros.*

# Queens Park Rangers F.C.
## Park Royal

*QPR v Plymouth Argyle*
Photo: Bowden Bros.

# Queens Park Rangers F.C.
## Park Royal

In *The Book of Football* article on QPR a rare mention of the club's grounds are included. Details of the move to 'the famous Kensal Rise Athletic Ground' are noted along with the financial problems that led them to leave and subsequently return at a higher rent. The author goes on to report that 'a lease was secured of the palatial ground at Park Royal, Willesden, a ground which for its possibilities is second to none in the kingdom'.

The claim is rather grand but the ground did have a good amount of cover and terracing. The map shows an oval arena which is presumed to be this ground. Also of interest is a further ground used by the club adjacent to Park Royal Station which is said to have been a copy of Middlesbrough's Ayresome Park. The *Britain From Above* website includes an image showing high banks but the grandstand had long since been demolished when the image was taken in 1930.

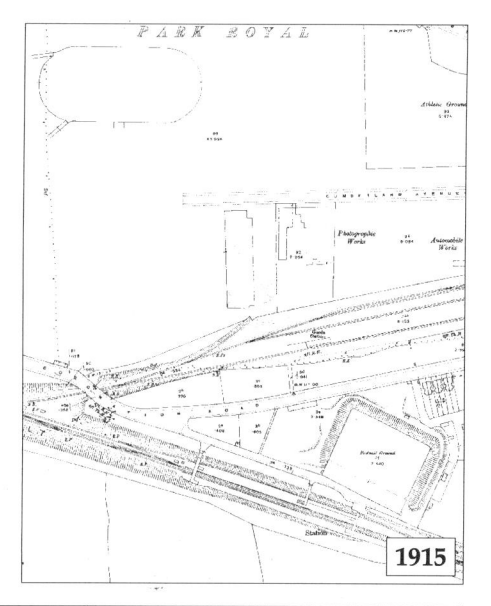

1915

*QPR v Plymouth Argyle*
*Photo*: Bowden Bros.

# Reading F.C.
## Elm Park

**Below**: *The Book of Football* caption for this image reads 'A capital view of Elm Park, Reading Football Club's enclosure, seen from the terraces opposite the stand.'

# Reading F.C.
## Elm Park

Elm Park in 1905 was a pleasant small ground. Today it seems remarkable that five years earlier a crowd of 10,000 crammed into the ground to see the F.A. Cup semi-final replay between Southampton and Millwall. At the time of the publication of *The Book of Football* the match did not event warrant a mention in the article on the club.

The atractive wooden stand on the Norfolk Road side survived until 1926 when high winds damaged it. At the time of construction clubs had yet to realise that it was best to avoid having their seated fans facing into the sun on bright days and the prevailing winds during bad weather.

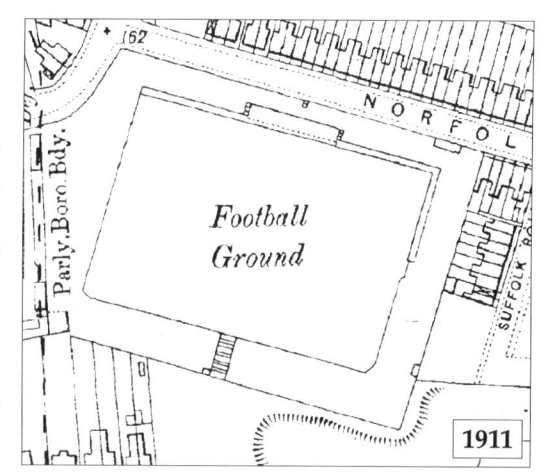

*Photo: W. Henry Dee, Reading*

*England v Scotland*
*Photo: Bowden Bros.*

# Sheffield United F.C.
## Bramall Lane

The caption for the photo on this page in *The Book of Football* reads 'Bramall Lane, Sheffield – the home of Sheffield United. One of the most famous League grounds in the kingdom.'

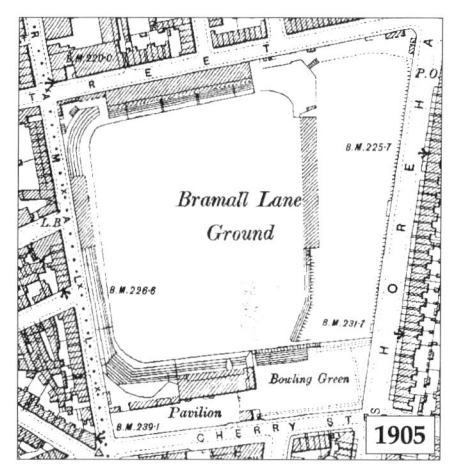

Bramall Lane served as both a football and cricket ground. The main stand was the first that Archibald Leitch built in England and opened in 1901. Simple in design, and already somewhat old-fashioned in appearance, the gabled press box is an impressive addition. Yorkshire CCC moved their headquarters from Bramall Lane in 1903 and football became the predominant sport at the ground. Cricket was played here until the redevelopment undertaken in 1973.

*Photo: Howard Barrett, Southwell*

# Sheffield United F.C.
## Bramall Lane

The two photos by Howard Barrett on this page would appear to have been taken at the same game. They were used as unrelated illustrations within an article on Football in London in *Association Football and The Men Who Made It*.

The image left is simply captioned as being the players Best and Lipsham. The scoreboard in the photo is the same one as seen in the photo on page 82 and so identifies the ground.

The lower image is captioned as being Birmingham v Sheffield United. It would seem that at this time the accepted way of writing the home team first had yet to be established, which can cause difficulties for historians. By looking at the images together it is possible to accurately identify both images.

Note that the cover over the Bramall Lane end as seen on page 82 had yet to be built when these photos were taken.

*Sheffield United v Birmingham City*
Photo: Howard Barrett, Southwell

*Sheffield United v Birmingham City*
Photo: Howard Barrett, Southwell

84

# Sheffield Wednesday F.C.
## Owlerton

Owlerton, known as Hillsborough since 1914, had been open for seven years when the image below was included in *The Book of Football* with the caption 'The Owlerton Ground, Sheffield Wednesday's famous football enclosure. The record attendance here was 36,413 SWFC v Portsmouth 18/2/05. The ground will hold about 50,000 persons.'

The stand on the far side is on the south side of the ground, the rear part having been brought from the club's previous ground, Olive Grove.

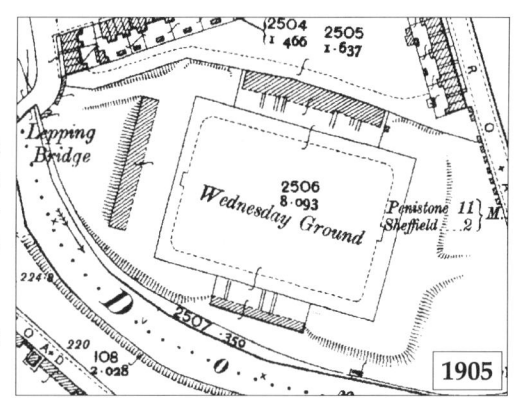

*Photo: Furniss, Sheffield*

# Southampton F.C.
## The Dell

**Below & opposite**: Brighton United were a short-lived club, the game illustrated being their first Southern League game. They did not see out their second season, although *The Book of Football* makes no mention of this.

The captions reads 'The Dell opened on September 3, 1898, when Southampton played Brighton United. The beauty of this ideal playing enclosure can be fully realised from the excellent photographs. On this historic occasion J. G. Fillings Esq., Mayor of Southampton, set the ball rolling by kicking-off for Brighton United in the first match on the new ground, perhaps the prettiest in the South.'

*Southampton v Brighton United*
Photo: F. G. O. Stuart, Southampton

# Southampton F.C.
## The Dell

Southampton were among the clubs in the South who challenged the domination of the Football League and F.A. Cup by clubs from the Midlands and the North. Their move to The Dell in 1898 was key to this and they were losing F.A. Cup finalists in 1900 and 1902.

Such was the importance of the club that even in 1906 *The Book of Football* regarded the photos on these pages and page 89 to be worthy of inclusion in the book despite being taken seven years before publication.

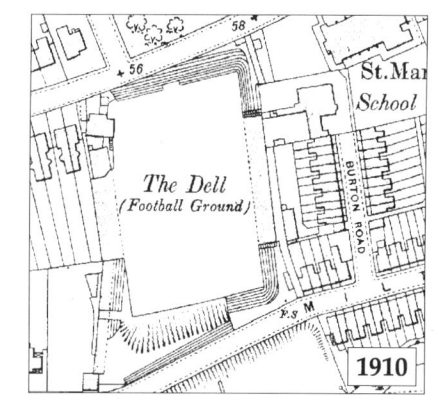

*Southampton v Brighton United*
*Photo: F. G. O. Stuart, Southampton*

# Southampton F.C.
## The Dell

**Top Left**: An uncaptioned image in *Association Football & The Men Who Made It*. The advert beyond the stand end is for French & Son, 40 Bedford Place. Remarkably the company are still trading at the same address to this day. The house in the far corner is the one casting a shadow across the pitch in the photo on page 89.

**Below, left**: The caption in *Association Football & The Men Who Made It* reads 'A throw in from touch – Bloomer receiving the ball' and identifies the opponents as Derby County. It is likely to be the F.A. Cup third round game played on 25 February 1899 when Southampton lost 1-2 to Derby County. It is probable that the photo top left is also taken at the same game.

Southampton F.C. 1905-6
Photo: F. G. O. Stuart, Southampton

88

*Southampton v Brighton United*
*Photo*: F. G. O. Stuart, Southampton

**Below**: This photo taken at White Hart Lane is probably the best action shot in the book, although I do wonder if the ball was subsequently placed in position in the darkroom.

*Tottenham Hotspur v Millwall*
*Photo*: Bowden Bros.

# Tottenham Hotspur F.C.
## White Hart Lane

The rise of professional football is well covered in *The Book of Football*, with Luton, Woolwich Arsenal, Millwall and Southampton's achievements all well detailed. The F.A. Cup win by Tottenham Hotspur as a Southern League side was a most significant step in the development of clubs in the South.

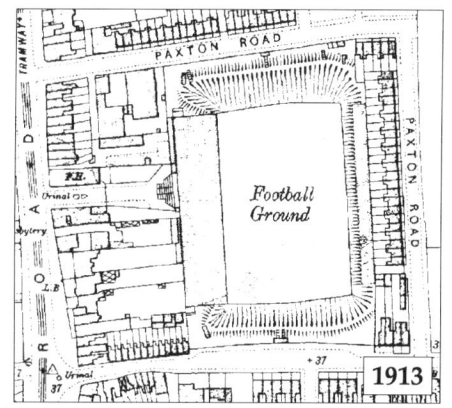

Photographers who took the photos at White Hart Lane in subsequent seasons give us a good impression of the ground but rarely took photos at the ends and so the main stand is not often shown. It hardly seems possible that the current Premier League ground could have grown from the ground we see here.

*Tottenham Hotspur v Millwall*
Photo: Bowden Bros.

# Tottenham Hotspur F.C.
## White Hart Lane

**Left**: An earlier image of the goal at the Park Lane end with houses on Paxton Road backing onto the East Terrace.

**Below, left**: *The Book of Football* caption reads 'A fine dribble by the Hotspur centre. Vivian Woodward in full flight.' The main stand can just be seen.

**Below**: A simple cover on the East Terrace side. This terrace was later uncovered until the East Stand was built which involved the demolition of the houses on Paxton Road.

*Tottenham Hotspur v Aston Villa*
Photo: Reinhold Thiele

Photo: Bowden Bros.

*Tottenham Hotspur v Millwall*
Photo: Bowden Bros.

92

# West Ham United F.C.
## The Boleyn Ground

The caption for this image in *The Book of Football* article on the club reads 'Boleyn Castle Ground, the historic home of West Ham United Football Club.'

The author details the problems the club had in attempting to extend their lease on their former home, the Memorial Ground. At one of the last games a Brother from the Boleyn Castle School was watching and suggested the club establish a ground at the school. Somehow the Home Office were involved and after an initial refusal the club were allowed to use the ground from 1904-5. Sadly no further details are included as to how the ground developed up to the taking of the photograph.

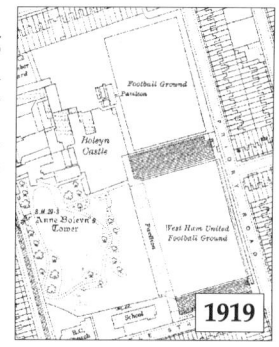

1919

Photo: J. E. Reeves, Canning Town

# Watford F.C.
## West Herts Ground

**Below**: The Watford F.C. players of season 1905-6 smartly dressed for their team photo.

*Photo: Bowden Bros.*

94

# Watford F.C.
## West Herts Ground

In 1906 Watford F.C. were playing at the West Herts Club Ground, also known as Cassio Road, which is still a recreation ground today. The club moved to Vicarage Road in 1922 having played League football at this ground for two years.

*The Book of Football* is full of praise for the ground saying 'the Cassio Road Ground is as near perfection as could be desired. Larger than Lords' Cricket Ground, just as level, beautifully drained and kept, the football portion is well-provided with a substantial club-house and stands.'

The map extract shows that the ground was two sided in terms of facilities for football spectators unlike other grounds which accommodated both football and cricket. This is likely to have been a major consideration when the club came to move.

The image right is a postcard with the end cover and stand seen behind the players. The photo opposite shows the end of the stand at the south of the ground alongside the pavilion.

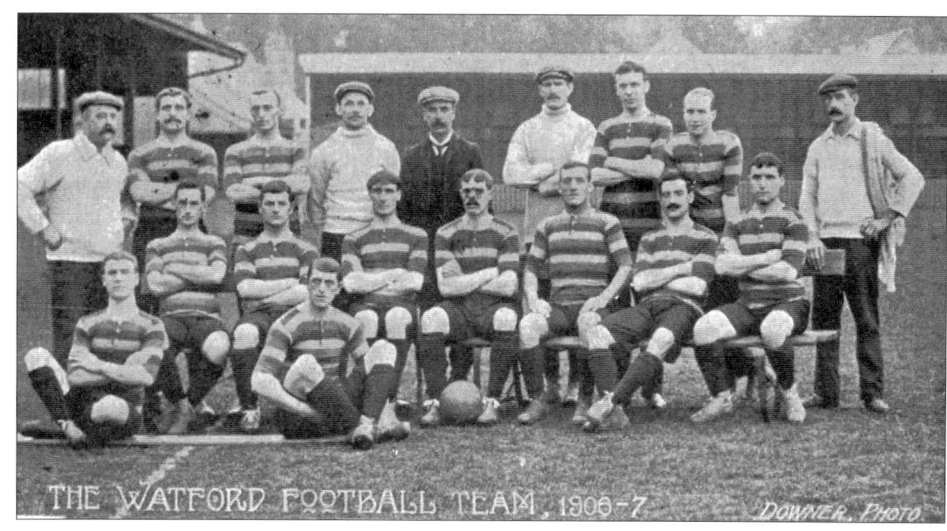

# West Bromwich Albion F.C.
## The Hawthorns

The *Book of Football* attempts to cover a range of topics including advice on playing the game. A sequence of images taken at the Hawthorns may inspire a young player but are of dubious worth. They are of interest as they show parts of the ground away from the main stand. *The Book of Football* identifies the player and states 'Simmons, the young West Bromwich player, shows how to pass the ball with the side of the foot. He is a clever and scientific exponent of the Association game.'

*Photo: Albert Wilkes*

*Photo: Albert Wilkes*

*Photo: Albert Wilkes*

*Photo: Albert Wilkes*

# West Bromwich Albion F.C.
## The Hawthorns

The *Book of Football* article on WBA by William McGregor includes details of every ground used by the club and the reasons for moving, the development etc other than the Hawthorns.

The main stand is shown to have numerous supports supporting the roof over the seats and paddock. This is probably in order that each support is smaller in section so as not to block the view from the seats as much as fewer but bigger supports would do.

*Photo: Albert Wilkes, West Bromwich*

# Wolverhampton Wanderers F.C.
## Molineux

*Association Football & The Men Who Made It* notes 'in 1899 the Wanderers left Dudley Road, and took up their quarters at the well-known headquarters of professional cycle racing, the Molineux Grounds.' Local industries included bicycle manufacturers, and in the late 1860s a cycle track had been built there by a local businessman.

Molineux House was at one end of ground, up a hill, with a bowling green overlooking the pitch. This can be seen as the flat area behind the goal in the action photo below.

<u>Below</u>: Wolverhampton Wanderers F.C. 1905-6. This team photo shows an interesting aspect of the design of the main stand. An enclosed space occupies one end and the solid timbers, which would not look out of place in an old barn, seem to allow a small area of cover behind the paddock area by the pitchside.

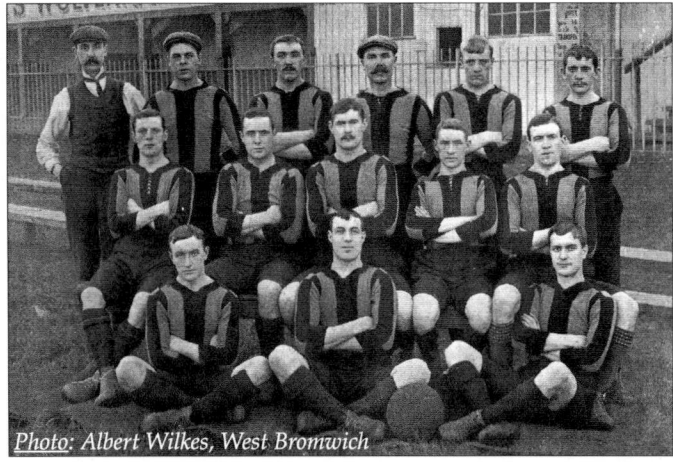

Wolverhampton Wanderers v Birmingham City

Photo: Albert Wilkes, West Bromwich

98

# Wolverhampton Wanderers F.C.
## Molineux

The image below of the Molineux Ground, Wolverhampton, is taken from the south end where the ground rises towards Molineux House. The caption for the image in *The Book of Football* reads 'The classic playing field of the Wolverhampton Wanderes Football Club.'

The end of the stand closest to the camera appears to be a glazed area with a gabled roof. In comparison to the present day the wide range of different approaches to designing and building stands in the early 1900s makes for interest in almost every photo from that time.

Photo: Arthur & Co.

# Woolwich Arsenal F.C.
## The Manor Ground, Plumstead

**Below**: Woolwich Arsenal F.C. are credited with first using Spion Kop as the name for a bank or terrace, a reference to a battle in the Boer War in 1900. They gave the name to the bank from which this image was taken, with the buildings of the Royal Arsenal at Woolwich behind.

# Woolwich Arsenal F.C.
## The Manor Ground, Plumstead

Woolwich Arsenal were the first club in the South to fully embrace professionalism and the first to join the Football League. Their stadium was developed into a good ground for the time, with covered stands on both sides of the pitch.

History may not have been fair to the Manor Ground, with poor attendances being cited as a reason for moving to Highbury. Photographers were regular visitors to the ground and their images show the ground with large crowds. Passions ran high and the club had to play elsewhere more than once following crowd trouble resulting in ground closures.

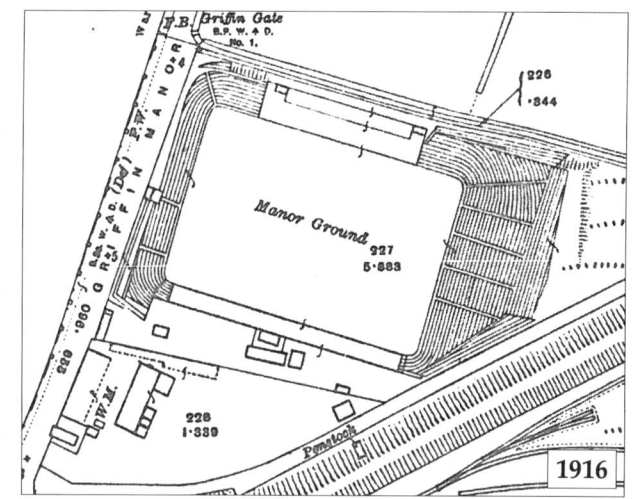

1916

*Woolwich Arsenal v Liverpool*
<u>Photo</u>: *Baker & Muggeridge*

# Woolwich Arsenal F.C.
## The Manor Ground, Plumstead

*Woolwich Arsenal F.C. 1905-6*
*Photo: E. G. Elbourne, Plumstead*

**Below, left and right**: *The Book of Football* captions for these images read 'Another view of the enclosure at Plumstead. The success of League football is plainly shown by the above photograph. A crowd such as this gathers in the sixpenny enclosure at Plumstead every other Saturday throughout the football season, and whatever discomfort the spectators suffer during the hour and a half that play lasts is completely forgotten in the excitement of the game. Though the ground at Plumstead has few claims to beauty, the densely packed crowd invariably presents a most impressive picture.'

*Woolwich Arsenal v Liverpool*
*Photo: Bowden Bros.*

*Woolwich Arsenal v Liverpool*
*Photo: Bowden Bros.*

# Woolwich Arsenal F.C.
## The Manor Ground, Plumstead

**Below**: The caption for this photo may have been exaggerating as *The Book of Football* says 'How severe was the Everton forward-line at one period of this match is clearly shown by the photograph above. Ashcroft is seen making a fine save at close quarters.'

*Woolwich Arsenal v Everton*
*Photo: Bowden Bros.*

**Index**: *Match action involving clubs in brackets*

Aldershot Military Stadium 33
Archibald Leitch 2, 5, 37, 40, 56, 63, 72, 83
Army 13, 33
Aston Villa 35-8, (18), (21-23), (50), (68), (70), (92)
Birmingham City 39, (84), (98)
Blackburn Rovers 40 (66)
Blackpool 41
Bolton Wanderers 42, 43, (1), (21)
Brentford 44
Brighton College 8, 9
Brighton United (86), (87), (89)
Bristol Rovers 45
Bury (50)
Cambridge University (10), (12), (13)
Cardiff Arms Park 31
Celtic (29)
Charterhouse School 9
Chelsea 48, 49
Chesterfield 47
Corinthian (11), (24)
Crystal Palace 1, 14 - 25
Derby County 50, 51, (14, 15), (36), (38), (68), (88)
England (16 - 18), (20), (82)
Everton 52, 53, (26), (27), (64, (68), (70), (103)
Fallowfield, Manchester 26, 27,
Forest School 6
Foulke, William 'Fatty' 19, 48, 49, 50
Fulham 54, 55, 56, (44)
Gillingham - see New Brompton
Grimsby Town 57
Hampden Park, Glasgow 28, 29
Leicester Fosse 58, 59

Liverpool (101), (102)
Luton Town 60. 61
Manchester City (1), (21)
Manchester United 62
Middlesbrough 63, (67)
Millwall 64 , (36), (38), (90 - 92)
Navy (13)
New Brompton 65
Newcastle United (18), (21 - 24)
Nottingham Forest 68, 69, 70
Notts County 66, 67
Oxford University (10, 12, 13)
Plymouth Argyle 74, 75, (78), (79)
Portsmouth 71 - 73, (60)
Preston North End (69)
Queen's Club 10 - 13
QPR 76, 77, 78, 79
Rangers (29)

Reading 80, 81
Scotland (16 - 18), (20), (82)
Sheffield United 82 - 84, (14, 15),
(19), (21), (42), (43), (50)
Sheffield Wednesday, 85
Southampton 86 - 89, (11)
Stoke City (57)
St Helens, Swansea 30
Third Lanark (29)
Tottenham Hotspur 90 - 92,
(19), (21), (42, 43),
West Ham United 93
West Bromwich Albion 96, 97
Westminster School 7
Wolverhampton Wanderers 98, 99,
(26), (27)
Woolwich Arsenal 100 - 103
Watford 94, 95

Finally, a quote from *Association Football and the Men Who Made It*: 'An enthusiast living in a country village in the New Forest once took his usual holidays in April instead of the summer. He was entitled to ten days in the year, and he had them. In that time he travelled about 600 miles and saw no less than five big football matches. Starting early on the Saturday, he reached Birmingham in time to see Aston Villa play Sunderland. On the Monday he went to Sheffield and watched the United and Blackburn Rovers*. On the Wednesday he witnessed a Lancashire Cup tie between Bury and Bolton Wanderers. Then he made his way to London and witnessed the English Cup Final between Notts (sic) Forest and Derby County, and finished up on the Monday with Woolwich Arsenal v Millwall.' Many of those reading this book will understand exactly why this fan undertook his trip! * *game actually played at Ewood Park not Bramall Lane.*